IMAGES
of England

CRYSTAL PALACE
FOOTBALL CLUB

IMAGES
of England

CRYSTAL PALACE
FOOTBALL CLUB

Compiled by
Revd Nigel Sands

TEMPUS

First published 1999
Copyright © Revd Nigel Sands, 1999

Tempus Publishing Limited
The Mill, Brimscombe Port,
Stroud, Gloucestershire, GL5 2QG

ISBN 0 7524 1544 1

Typesetting and origination by
Tempus Publishing Limited
Printed in Great Britain by
Midway Clark Printing, Wiltshire

Other Sporting Titles from Tempus:

Anfield Voices
Bury FC
Bristol Rovers FC
Cardiff City FC 1899-1947
Cardiff City FC 1947-1971
Cardiff RFC
Charlton Athletic FC
Exeter City FC
Glamorgan CCC
Leeds RLFC
Leeds United FC
Llanelli RFC
Newport County FC 1912-1960
Oxford United FC
Plymouth Argyle FC 1886-1986
Reading FC
Roker Park Voices
Sheffield United FC
Sunderland FC
Surrey CCC
Tranmere Rovers FC
Yorkshire CCC

Contents

Introduction

I am delighted to be able to offer this pictorial history of Crystal Palace FC to the club and its supporters for, as many Eagles fans know very well, the Palace have been my team through thick and thin for what now amounts to substantially more than fifty years (and, believe me, there were some times when things were so thin that any recent difficulties and frustrations at Selhurst Park seem almost balmy by comparison). Equally, during the last twenty-five years as a regular contributor to the matchday programme and as the club's historian, I have grown familiar with the stories and personnel from Palace's days before the Second World War. Thus it is a pleasure to be able to introduce the stars and key club officials of those times to present-day supporters, or to reacquaint them with their admirers who followed the club as their contemporaries.

Nigel Sands
Honorary Chaplain and club historian
Crystal Palace FC
January 1999

Mark Goldberg became Palace's thirteenth chairman on 5 June 1998 and will carry the club's hopes forward into the new millennium.

One
Foundation and Early Progress 1905-24

Crystal Palace Football Club, 1909/10 season. From left to right, back row: J. Moult, J. Hughes, H. Collyer, C. Clark, C. Bradley, F. Lee, Mr E. Goodman (Secretary/Manager). Third row: R. Spottiswood, Mr A. Birch (Trainer), W. Higgins, J. Johnson, J. Bulcock, H. Hanger, W. Goodhind, ? Taylor. Second row: G. Garrett, G. Payne, G. Woodger, J.W. Williams, M. Griffin, E. Myers. Front row: R. Gibson, A. Haywood, J. Hullock, A. Wilson.

This panoramic view of the Crystal Palace shows just what a magnificent venue it was for a football ground. The low-level Crystal Palace station is to the left of the arena, at which twenty FA Cup finals were staged between 1895 and 1914 and where the Palace club played almost all its home games.

A youthful Edmund Goodman. Mr Goodman was Palace's secretary from the club's foundation until 1933 and managed the playing team from 1907 to 1925. He joined Palace from Aston Villa when our club's founders sought Villa's help in setting up the new team. It was as a result of Villa's warm response, as well as Mr Goodman's high regard for them, that the Palace adopted Villa's colours of claret and blue shirts and white shorts. Palace have usually kept to some derivative form of kit ever since.

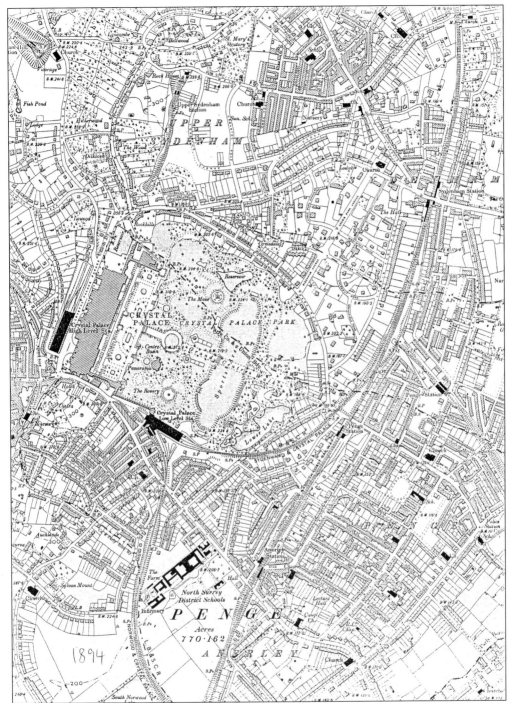

The 1894 Ordnance Survey map sets the Crystal Palace building and its grounds within the surrounding locality. It is interesting to compare landmarks in the photograph opposite with their position on this map. Perhaps there are modern day Palace fans, who live in the area shown on this map of over a hundred years ago, who can identify the situation of their homes on it?

During the closing years of his cricketing career, the legendary W.G. Grace had several connections in South London and at the Crystal Palace. With typical confidence in his ability, 'WG' put himself forward to manage the new Crystal Palace Football Club in 1905, but was turned down. It must have been one of the very few occasions in his illustrious sporting career that someone was preferred ahead of him!

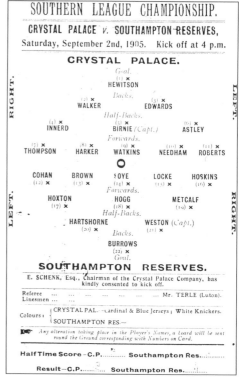

The programme for Palace's inaugural match in the Southern League. Palace led 3-0 within the first half hour…but went down 3-4. However, we didn't lose another match in that competition all season and won the Southern League Division Two championship, in a thrilling finish, over close rivals Leyton.

In what was only Palace's second season, 1906/07, they had a quite superb FA Cup run. Perhaps the club's greatest result of all time was gained in the (old) first round, when The Glaziers won at Newcastle. They followed this with wins over strong Southern League sides Fulham and Brentford. This cartoon shows the confidence with which Palace approached the quarter-final against Everton! However, the bubble burst and Palace went out 0-4 in a Goodison Park replay.

Some rare photographic action from the Southern League. The game is being played at the Crystal Palace during the Festival of Empire staged there. It is Saturday 16 September 1911 and the opponents are Southern League champions Swindon Town. Harry Hanger (light shirt, off the ground) heads for goal, while behind him, to the right, is the visitors' great England international of the period – Harold Fleming. The face of Palace centre half Jimmy Hughes can be seen between the two players on Hanger's left. The match ended 2-2, after both teams had taken the lead at some point in the game. Palace finished the season seventh in the Southern League and Swindon finished fourth.

The following four pictures are wonderfully evocative of the age in which they were taken and represent the early heroes of Crystal Palace Football Club. Notice the ankle-deep boots, the studs and the toe caps. The ball is laced and the leather untreated, so it would invariably absorb moisture from a wet or damp pitch, thereby becoming extremely heavy and slippery as soap. It is also intriguing to note that the fashion of the day was for 'jerseys', as they were called, to be worn outside the (knee-length) shorts. All four of these players were key men in Palace's inaugural season. Wilfred Innerd (left) became Palace's captain in 1906. He was seldom absent from the early Palace sides until he was badly hurt in the tremendous FA Cup victory over Wolves in January 1909. He played 111 Southern League matches for Crystal Palace Football Club.

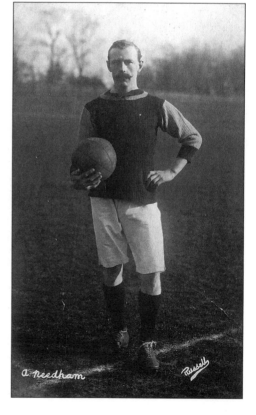

Versatile Archie Needham (right) appeared at inside forward, full back and on both wings – but his biggest impact was as a goalscorer. He hit twenty Southern League goals in 1905/06, to ensure the divisional title and holds a permanent place in the Palace hall of fame for the decisive strike that knocked out FA Cup-holders Wolverhampton Wanderers in a thrilling replay at the Crystal Palace in January 1909.

Horace Astley (right) usually played at right half, but also occasionally (and effectively) at centre forward. He spent two seasons with the Palace, but will always be remembered as the man whose goal beat the Football League Champions (and previous season's finalists) Newcastle at Gallowgate in the FA Cup (old) first round in January 1907.

Bob Hewitson (left) was a goalkeeper ('keepers didn't wear distinctive jerseys then) who joined The Glaziers from Barnsley and played seventy-five consecutive Southern League and cup games, before joining Oldham in 1907. He returned to South London in 1909 to play for Croydon Common, after a spell with Tottenham.

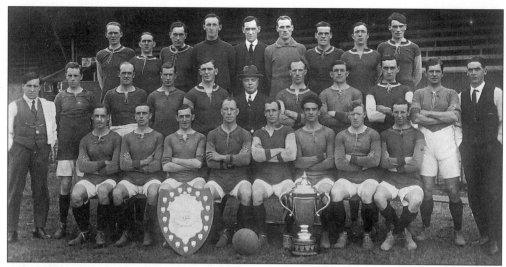

Upon Palace's election to the Football League for the 1920/21 season, the club immediately won promotion to Division Two. Here are the players who made that tremendous achievement possible, along with the Division Three Championship Shield and the London Challenge Cup, which they also won that season. From left to right, back row: Joe Nixon, Albert Harry, F. King, Jack Alderson, Arthur Swift (Assistant Trainer), George Irwin, Jimmy Allen, Bill Hand, Harry Dreyer. Middle row: W. Jones (Trainer), Roy McCracken, 'Tom' Jones, Andrew Kennedy, Albert Feebury, Mr Edmund Goodman (Manager), Albert Wells, Ernie Rhodes, J. Collier, Jack Little, A. Greig (Assistant Trainer). Front row: Ben Bateman, Tom Storey, John Conner, Ted Smith, Alf Wood, Bert Menlove, John Cartwright, John Whibley.

Presented with FOOTBALL SPECIAL, October 21st, 1922.

JACK ALDERSON
keeps the ball out of
the Crystal Palace goal.
Comes from Crook, and
played for Newcastle
when quite a lad.
Height, 6 ft.   Weight,
12 st. 4 lbs.

OUR
FOOTBALL
BOYS—
No. 10.

Jack Alderson was Palace's goalkeeper throughout the 1920/21 Division Three Championship campaign: indeed he was the first-choice custodian from 1919 until 1924. He was a huge favourite with the supporters and gained applause and admiration at many away grounds for his displays. Like all the best goalkeepers, he improved with age and, in his last season with Palace, became a remarkable penalty saver. He thoroughly deserved the single international honour he received when he represented England against France in Paris on 10 May 1923.

16

Jack Little was Palace's first choice right-back for seven seasons after the resumption of competitive football following the hiatus of the First World War. However, he was already well known to local football fans, having been a regular member of the Croydon Common side which had won promotion in 1913/14. Jack will be forever associated, in Palace's history, with the other members of the fabulous defensive triumvirate of Alderson, Little and 'Dusty' Rhodes – who played an amazing sequence of exactly 100 consecutive matches together in the years after the First World War. It is worth noting that over half of Jack's 242 League appearances for Palace were made in Division Two of the Football League.

George Whitworth was a brave, strong centre forward. He had 'guested' for Palace effectively during the First World War and played well (and indeed scored) for Northampton against us after it, so, when manager Edmund Goodman needed a quality striker in March 1922, he acted quickly and decisively. George's first Football League appearance for Palace was up at Bury, where he equalised before the break, hit the bar soon after it and then set up Ben Bateman for the winner – some debut! His aptitude and style can be measured by the fans of today from the fact that he scored forty-eight Division Two goals for Palace between 1922 and 1925, at a time when the club were far from being a great side. It is worth bearing in mind that, in the higher divisions, that tally has only been bettered at our club by Mark Bright and Ian Wright.

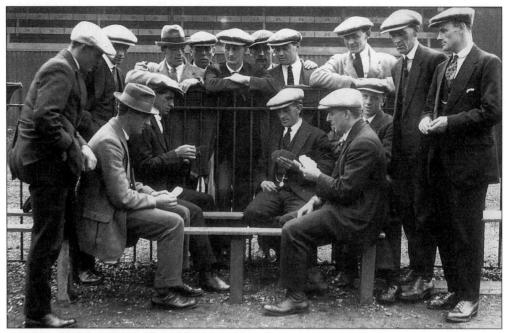

A group of Palace players relax with a game of cards at The Nest in the mid-1920s. Some things in football never change!

Here's another Palace hero of the 1920s – tall, balding, Welsh international centre half, J.T. Jones, known to his friends as 'Tom'. He joined Palace from Stoke City in 1920 and was a key member of our defence in the 1920/21 championship season, going on to score a fabulous headed goal in the club's first match in Division Two – a 4-1 win against highly fancied visitors Nottingham Forest. He left the club in the summer of 1922, having played in sixty-six League and cup games and scored six goals.

Two
Palace on the Move
1924-39

Crystal Palace Football Club, 1926/27 season. From left to right, back row: W. Jones (Trainer), H. Pettit, ? Donachie, E. Holmes, T. Crosskey, W. Grant, S. Tonner, J. Cartwright (Assistant Trainer). Middle row: W. Callender, J. Nixon, L. Smith, J. Hamilton, P. Cherrett, R. Orr, G. Clarke, C. Blakemore, T. Coyle. Front row: H. Gallagher, R. Greener, C. Cross, Mr A. Maley (Manager), Mr E. Goodman (Secretary), Mr L. Goodman (Assistant Secretary), C. Hilley, V. Barnes, H. Hopkins. On the ground: J. Flood, W. Turner, A. Harry.

Selhurst Park. The CRYSTAL PALACE F. Club's new ground. Opened by the Lord Mayor of London Sat Aug 30th. 1924. Gate 20,000. CRYSTAL PALACE. 0. SHEFFIELD WED'Y. 1.

This picture of Selhurst Park, taken on Saturday 30 August 1924, will look fairly familiar to most readers, but several details are very interesting. Given that at least one team is 'kicking-in', it is obvious that the late crush at the turnstiles is by no means a modern phenomenon. Several, now distinguished, Palace fans have claimed to be amongst the children peering through the corrugated iron gates for a glimpse of the spectacle – but no one has yet laid claim to owning the bicycle!

In the match that followed the congestion shown above, Sheffield Wednesday did not have matters all their own way, despite their 1-0 victory. Teddy Davison is seen here punching a shot from a Palace raid over the bar of the Holmesdale Road goal.

Jim Mercer's cartoon captures some of the highlights of Palace's FA Cup exploits during the late 1920s – notably the great victory over Chelsea, at which the Selhurst Park record attendance was established (and remained so for the next forty years).

The Crystal Palace Football Club has usually been extremely well served by its goalkeepers. The two featured on this page are no exception, both being fine pre-war players for the club. Billy Callender (left) strikes a nonchalant pose by the goalpost. He was quite superb, as well as being hugely popular, during his Palace career of 225 League and cup games between 1926 and 1932.

Ronnie Dunn (right) made 175 Palace appearances between 1931 and 1936. He was a former Guardsman who was spotted in an Army representative game at Selhurst Park in 1929. He was an ideal successor to the brilliant Callender but, regrettably, the Palace sides of the early and mid-1930s were so modest that his prowess was only appreciated by Palace fans of the period, rather than those of bigger clubs, as he deserved.

The caricature is of Sydney Bourne, who was Palace's first chairman and remains the longest serving holder of that office. He was one of the men who helped establish the club and set it on the way to success. Invited to join the Palace board by Edmund Goodman, Sydney was elected chairman at the club's first board meeting and remained in office until his death in 1930. He was highly thought of throughout his tenure and, when he died, the flag was flown at half-mast the following afternoon, when Palace trounced Newport County 7-1 – giving him just the sort of farewell he would have wished.

MR. SYDNEY BOURNE.

AN OLD FAVOURITE—" CHARLEY'S AUNT." (Not at the New Theatre)

"STILL RUNNING"—AND KEEPING UP A HOT PACE TOO.

The Palace programme of the 1920s and 1930s often carried a topical cartoon. This one is taken from the 1930/31 season, when Palace and Northampton pushed Notts County hard (but ultimately unsuccessfully) for the Division Three (South) title and the single promotion place into Division Two.

This, and the following page, represents a tribute to Palace's exciting wingers in the inter-war years. Albert Harry (left) was a diminutive, bow-legged character whose talent on the right flank drew praise from every quarter and made him a household name in Palace-supporting areas for at least half a century. Albert played 440 senior matches for Palace between 1922 and 1934, contributing markedly to such successes as we gained in that period.

George Clarke was a flame-haired, goalscoring left-winger, who starred for the Palace between 1925 and 1933. He was a ball player with real craft, but also fast and clever, with a lethal shot – skills which have etched his name for all time in the Palace annals. He remains, to this day, one of the club's top five marksmen – his tally of 106 goals is way ahead of that of any other Palace winger – yet his major contribution was to supply chances for the centre forwards! George Clark was truly a prince amongst Palace wingers.

Jim Mercer's cartoon extends the range of subjects for us in his uniquely attractive style.

'Jimmy' Wilde was tall, slim and totally dominating at centre half. He was a regular from 1928/29 for eight full seasons and club captain for six of those. In his debut season, Palace were pipped for the single promotion place by Charlton Athletic, who won it on goal average alone in the most exciting finish to a Division Three season ever seen at our club. Jimmy went on to become recognised as one of the most accomplished half-backs in Palace's section and would produce constructive, driving performances from either wing-half berth when required to do so.

Peter Simpson is still Palace's all-time leading goalscorer and seems likely to remain so. He joined the club in 1929 and notched a hat-trick on his debut. He was a famed and feared striker in the Palace colours for over six seasons, scoring 165 League and cup goals from just 195 appearances. However, Peter was more than just a goal machine – his distributive skills were prodigious. After finishing his career with West Ham and Reading, he took on a shop in West Croydon. Peter died in 1974 but, at Crystal Palace FC at least, he is immortal.

Tom Bromilow.

Tom Bromilow, a former Liverpool and England wing-half, was Palace's manager from 1935 until 1939. He brought the club closer to promotion into Division Two than any other incumbent in a span of thirty-five years, when his Palace team missed out, by three points, to Newport County in 1938/39. He was well-liked and respected at Selhurst Park and when he left, for Leicester City, he did so on good terms and with the knowledge he had done his job well.

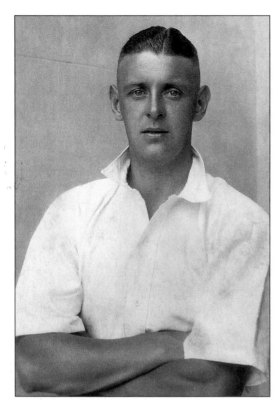

This pair of Palace defenders, from the late 1930s, epitomise the teak-tough professional footballers of that period. George Walker (left) was tall, strong, a former Scottish international and Palace's captain from 1936 until 1939. Playing at centre half, he rarely missed a game until midwinter 1938/39, when he was badly injured and unable to play for the club again.

Fred Gregory joined Palace from Reading in December 1937. He was a dependable full-back – who occasionally became an exciting, battering-ram centre forward! He had an immensely powerful free kick and was very strong. During 1938/39 he netted five goals in two games when drafted in up front early in the season, including a hat-trick on 1 October against Clapton Orient.

Three
Sirens at Selhurst
1939-46

Crystal Palace Football Club, 1939/40 season. From left to right, back row: D. Kearns (Ground Staff), D. Jordan, A. Robson, A. Hudgell, F. Dawes, R. Greener (Assistant Trainer), E. Owens, N. Collins, W. Roberts, A. Wilson, V. Carter (Ground Staff), C. Catlett (Groundsman). Middle row: T. Reece, L. Lievesley, F. Wright, F. Gregory, A. Tootill, A. Chesters, R. Shanks, J. Lewis, M. Gregory, J. Blackman, A. James. Front row: Mr G. Irwin (Manager), Messrs F. Broomfield, F. Young and R. Blaxill (Directors), Mr E. Truett (Chairman), Messrs R. Cornell and P. Harper (Directors), Mr F. Burrell (Secretary), Dr J. Jones (Medical Officer). Seated: E. Waldron, T. Smith, I. Gillespie, W. Bark.

Sporting Yesterdays

Jim Mercer's cartoon ably depicts some of the wartime scenes at Selhurst Park. The air-raid sirens' wail became a feared and hated sound for everyone, but it certainly sharpened up wartime football because it brought an immediate end to a match, whatever stage it may have reached – the score at that point becoming the final result – or prevented any play at all.

The Second World War spoilt the careers of hundreds of fine footballers. Here are two of them that played for Crystal Palace. Albert Wilson (right) was a speedy, powerful winger, who joined the Palace in January 1939. He netted on his debut then went on to help Palace to several wartime honours, before being transferred to Rotherham prior to the start of the 1946/47 season.

Fred Dawes (left) was the only Palace player to make 100 appearances on either side of the Second World War and was as fine and loyal a servant as the club has ever had. But for the war, his 237 first class games in our (various) colours could have reached an astonishing figure, but he is remembered by fans of the period as being honest, hardworking, clean and a credit to both his profession and the club.

Here's a rare action shot from a wartime football match. Palace (in black and white) are at home to Aldershot on Saturday 16 March 1940 and are conceding The Shots' third goal – after just ten minutes play! Nevertheless, Palace had sufficient chances to remedy matters, but did not do so. Fred Gregory failed with his two penalties (taken within minutes of each other), although he then scored with a great free kick, before Albert Robson further reduced the deficit. Aldershot extended their lead mid-way through the second half and Palace finished the scoring with a third penalty, which Fred Gregory this time converted. Fred is the Palace number two in the picture and our goalkeeper is Fred Tootill. The background to this picture should be of considerable interest to local people.

CRYSTAL PALACE FOOTBALL CLUB

President :—Sir Adam Maitland, M.P.
Directors :—Messrs. P. S. Harper (Chairman), F. J. Young (Vice-Chairman), F. Broomfield, G. J. Ellis, E. T. Truett.
Secretary-Manager :—G. W. Irwin.
NEAREST STATIONS : NORWOOD JUNCTION, SELHURST, and THORNTON HEATH.
Bus Services—133, 68, 75 ; 654 (Trolley).

OFFICIAL PROGRAMME

No. 2. Vol. LV.   SEASON 1944-45

Saturday, Sept. 9th, 1944.   Kick-off 3.15 p.m.   Price : ONE PENNY

CRYSTAL PALACE

RIGHT WING.   LEFT WING

1
TOOTILL
Goal

2   3
MOUNTFORD   DAWES (F.)
Right Back   Left Back

4   5   6
BURKE   MILLBANKS   LIEVESLEY
Right Half   Centre Half   Left Half

7   8   9   10   11
DRIVER   DAWES (A.)   ROBINSON   LEWIS (G.)   WILSON
Outside Right Inside Right Centre Forward Inside Left Outside Left

Referee : A. S. MELTON   Linesmen :—
                                                        Blue Flag : G. M. JARVIS.
(New Barking)   Red Flag : W. HOWARD.

11   10   9   8   7
STEPHENS   READ   HODGES   WILSON   HASSELL
Outside Left Inside Left Centre Forward Inside Right Outside Right

6   4
WINNING   NEEDHAM   REECE
Left Half   Centre Half   Right Half

3   2
STEER   RISTON
Left Back   Right Back

1
FAIRHURST
(Goal)

LEFT WING   RIGHT WING

BRIGHTON

Next Saturday: **CHELSEA RES.** (3.15)   London War Combination.
Saturday, 23rd: **FULHAM RES.** (3.15)   London War Combination.

The single-sheet matchday programme for a game in the penultimate wartime season, 1944/45. Palace won the game 5-2. Note the appearance of two brothers in the Palace side: Fred and Albert Dawes.

"WOT, NO GOALS?". I. HARDING

For the last wartime season, the Crystal Palace Supporters' Club produced a lively, interesting and informative matchday programme of eight pages. This often included a contemporary cartoon and a player caricature – examples of both are shown on this page. The drawing (above) refers to the intensely exciting FA Cup tie, played at Selhurst Park on Wednesday 9 January 1946, against Queens Park Rangers in a deluge on a quagmire of a pitch. The game ended goal-less, despite the playing of extra time. The replay was staged at Fulham, where Rangers won 1-0.

Douglas Graham

Goalkeeper Dick Graham (left) was perhaps the best signing made by wartime manager George Irwin. He had 'guested' for the Palace earlier in the 1945/46 season, but signed in time to appear in the match against Queens Park Rangers referred to above. Dick was to become a fine goalkeeper, who was both brave and stylish, before his playing career was beset, and prematurely ended, by a recurring back injury. However, read on, because Dick's greatest contribution to the Palace was yet to come!

Four
Forties, Fifties and the Fourth Division 1946-60

Crystal Palace Football Club, 1955/56. This is a typical line-up from the season. From left to right, back row: Don Moss, Len Choules, Roy Bailey, Jack Saunders, Alf Noakes, Jim Sanders. Front row: Ron Brett, Jimmy Belcher, Mike Deakin, George Cooper, Peter Berry.

The post-war action shots on this page were first published in the 1947/48 *Club Handbook*, edited by Des Beamish, a most loyal Palace fan for over sixty years. *Above*: Goalkeeper Dick Graham jumps to field a high ball as Watford attack the Holmesdale Road goal on Saturday 27 September 1947. Also in the picture are Palace defenders (from left to right) Jack Lewis, Bill Bassett and Ted Harding. Palace lost 1-2, to the disappointment of the impressive (almost 17,000) crowd. *Left*: Dick is under pressure again, but appears to have safely dealt with this attack.

Former England centre forward Tommy Lawton (left), the player/manager of Notts County, is greeted by Palace skipper Fred Dawes, prior to the match at Selhurst Park on Saturday 10 September 1949, which was played in front of 26,847 excited fans. Palace put up a fine show against the division's top scorers at the time (County went on to become champions) and prevented Lawton from finding the net himself, although they went down by the odd goal in three.

Ronnie Rooke was appointed as Palace's player/manager in 1949. He was a great personality in London football at that time and had been a prolific goalscorer for his previous clubs, Arsenal and Fulham, whom he had joined from the Palace in 1936. He took Palace to their best post-war season in Division Three (South) in 1949/50, but the following term was disastrous and he left in November 1951.

Albert Foulds was a powerful centre forward, recruited for Palace from Rochdale in the summer of 1953. He scored four goals in seventeen Division Three (South) appearances, before moving back north to Crewe.

The board of directors who took over the Crystal Palace Football Club in early 1950. From left to right, back row: Guy Robson, Ralph Shrager, Colonel Jack Trevor, John Dunster. Front row: Arthur Wait, David Harris, Victor Ercolani. The men were all long-established friends and Palace fans. Principally under the chairmanships of Arthur Wait (in particular) and John Dunster, they provided the club with such new vitality and ambition that its destiny would be transformed. The portrait behind the group is of the club's president, F.J. Nettlefold.

Polished, intelligent, international full-back Laurie Scott, from Arsenal, was in charge of affairs at Crystal Palace from October 1951 to September 1954. His debut as Palace boss was watched by 21,000 fans, Palace winning 3-1 against Ipswich.

Harry McDonald, who played 146 League and cup games for Palace in the early 1950s, was a strong, sturdy left-back. He always appeared immaculate and unruffled, with composed and controlled performances to match.

Cam Burgess had joined the Palace from Chester a few weeks before the arrival of Laurie Scott and had an explosive, if brief, career with the club. He hit twenty-one League goals from just twenty-two outings in 1951/52 and nineteen from twenty-five in the next season, including a fabulous run of three hat-tricks in four games and twelve goals in six matches, during the autumn.

Palace's Bob Thomas bears down on Southend goalkeeper Harry Threadgold during the match between the two clubs at Selhurst Park on Saturday 20 March 1954. Bob was clearly unsuccessful on this occasion, but he was on target twice in Palace's 4-2 win.

Les Devonshire played as a winger and as an inside forward for the Palace in the first half of the 1950s, making eighty-seven League and cup appearances and scoring twelve goals. He also persuaded prolific striker Cam Burgess (see previous page) of the wisdom of moving to Selhurst Park and was instrumental in many of his friend's goals for us.

Torquay United had the opportunity of promotion from Division Three (South) at the end of 1956/57. To do so, they had to beat the Palace at Selhurst Park in the last game of the season. Unfortunately for the 1,500 fans that had come up from Devon for the Wednesday evening match, they could only draw 1-1. This picture shows Vic Rouse collecting the ball, with Tony Collins (who joined the Palace six months later) challenging and Jack Edwards in close attendance.

Tall, lean, versatile defender Len Choules starred for the Palace for ten seasons, after making his debut at Ipswich in April 1953. He accumulated 280 senior appearances so that, even today, he remains comfortably amongst Palace's top twenty in the all-time lists. Len's height and adroit heading ability also made him a useful occasional striker, whilst his mop of unruly, fair hair meant that he could always be picked out, even when in the thick of the action.

43

Peter Berry was another versatile player. During the mid-1950s, he played effectively at outside right, inside forward and centre forward. Although he wasn't a great goalscorer, he was an intelligent, thoughtful player. Altogether, Peter made 161 Palace appearances and scored twenty-eight goals, before Sir Alf Ramsey signed him for Ipswich Town in 1958.

Mike Deakin, a mobile, resourceful centre forward, was manager Cyril Spiers' first signing for Palace in November 1954 and was certainly among our best players in the trying years in which he was with the club. For example, he hit a hit-trick at Southend in October 1955 (although Palace still contrived to lose the game!) and he notched twenty-three goals from thirty-four Division Four appearances in 1958/59.

CRYSTAL PALACE F.C.

OFFICIAL PROGRAMME – Threepence

No. 14   Tuesday, 25th December, 1956

The front cover of the Palace programme for the Christmas Day game against Queens Park Rangers in 1956 – the last time that Selhurst Park hosted a match on the festival itself. Palace won 2-1, with goals from Jim Belcher and Barry Pierce in the last eight minutes.

Despite the occasional glimmer of hope, the Palace were not in serious contention for a place in the new, national Division Three at the end of 1957/58. Manager Cyril Spiers' final ploy to galvanise the team was to sign Johnny McNichol from Chelsea, just before the transfer deadline. Johnny scored on his debut to earn Palace a 1-0 win over visiting Port Vale (the match from which this action shot is taken), but even his distinguished presence was not sufficient to spare Palace from entering the new League basement of Division Four.

Palace's first game in Division Four was at home to Crewe Alexandra on Saturday 23 August 1958 and the match provided gripping entertainment, the Palace eventually winning 6-2, despite the fact that Crewe had opened the scoring. This picture shows Palace winger Bernard Harrison menacing Alexandra's goalkeeper, Jerry Lowry.

Five

From the Fourth to the First 1960-69

Crystal Palace Football Club, 1963/64. This is a promotion-winning line-up, whose 2-2 draw at Wrexham on Wednesday 22 April 1964 was sufficient to ensure Division Two football. From left to right, back row: Bert Howe, Alan Stephenson, Bill Glazier, Brian Wood, Terry Long, George Petchey. Front row: Bobby Kellard, Dickie Dowsett, Cliff Holton, Brian Whitehouse, Eddie Werge.

Left: Manager Arthur Rowe. *Right*: Johnny McNichol, the captain of Palace's 1960/61 promotion-winning team.

Action from the early-season fixture against Hartlepool United at Selhurst Park, which finished 2-2. The Palace men (wearing hooped shirts) seeking their way through the massed ranks of the visitors' defence are, from left to right: Roy Summersby, Johnny Byrne and George Petchey.

Palace *v.* Watford in the FA Cup second round on Saturday 26 November 1960. Watching Denis Uphill toe-poke a shot past the opposing centre half, in front of a perfectly placed referee, are, from left to right: Johnny Byrne, Roy Summersby and Ron Heckman.

Johnny Byrne gets his shot in too, despite being closely marked in the match. [Both of these pictures come from the Rob Marsden collection.]

Two of Palace's goals in the 7-2 rout of Torquay on Saturday 16 December 1961. *Above:* Johnny Byrne watches a header from Denis Uphill beat The Gulls' goalkeeper, Eddie Ward [Rob Marsden collection]. *Below left:* Ward is left clawing the air in a vain attempt to thwart Uphill's powerful drive. *Below right:* Johnny Byrne was the inspiration of Palace's promotion side of 1960/61 and was idolised by the fans.

Crystal Palace *v*. Real Madrid. The Spanish maestros paid their first visit to London to celebrate the opening of Palace's new floodlights on Wednesday 18 April 1962. Here, Terry Long, Roy Summersby and Johnny Byrne watch Brian Wood provide stern opposition for Real's Alfredo di Stefano.

Terry Long's smashing drive hurtles into Real's net, to make the score 3-4 and set up a fabulous finish to this wonderful night. However, there was to be no further scoring.

Palace at Brighton on Saturday 12 January 1963. This was a rare match that just beat the beginning of the 'big freeze' of the 1962/63 winter. Palace, under new manager Dick Graham, took full advantage and won 2-1. Cliff Holton (centre, wearing pale gloves) is firing in a shot, despite the attentions of the Albion defender.

Palace came within seconds of holding Division One Aston Villa to a 3-3 draw in the FA Cup third round tie at Villa Park on Saturday 6 January 1962. Here is the line-up of heroes on that afternoon, from left to right, back row: Terry Long, Roy Summersby, George Petchey, Vic Rouse, Brian Wood, Johnny McNichol. Front row: Ronnie Allen, Johnny Byrne, Denis Uphill, John Cartwright, Ron Heckman.

52

Palace secured promotion, for the second time in three years, in April 1964. The final match of the season was against Oldham (a 1-3 defeat) at Selhurst Park. In this shot, Brian Wood is putting in a header, despite the attentions of two Latics defenders. Brian Whitehouse is the player supporting him.

Palace fans, in the foreground, cheer their heroes as they appear in the directors' box after the Oldham game. This side took the Palace back to the higher divisions after an absence of thirty-nine years.

The squad of players, plus the officials and directors of Crystal Palace FC, as they prepare for Division Two duty (for the first time since 1925) in August 1964. From left to right, back row: R. Kellard, R. Allen, R. Horobin, P. Cutler, F. Lucas, P. Barrett, A. Howe, J. Sewell, W. Fuller, P. Burridge, S. Imlach, M. Griffiths, W. Birch. Middle row: R. Sayer, P. Skinner, E. Werge, T. Long, B. Whitehouse, A. Stephenson, W. Glazier, J. Holsgrove, J. Jackson, C. Holton, D. Townsend, B. Wood, D. Dowsett, C. Catlett (Groundsman), J. Willard (Trainer). Front row: Miss S. Scoble, C. Hassell (Secretary), Mr D. Graham (Manager), Mr R. Shrager (Director), Mr A. Wait (Chairman), Messrs J. Dunster and V. Ercolani (Directors), Mr A. Rowe (Assistant Manager), Mrs M. Hutchings.

These two pictures show the pair of goalkeepers who dominated the 1960s at Crystal Palace. *Left*: Bill Glazier played 113 games for Palace between 1962 and 1964, before moving to Coventry City for £35,000 (a record fee for a goalkeeper at that time). *Right*: John Jackson was Glazier's successor. 'Jacko' made a hugely significant contribution to the 1968/69 promotion, as an ever-present member of the team. Jackson went on to become absolutely outstanding in the top flight and accumulated 393 senior Palace appearances between 1964 and 1973.

Centre half John McCormick was another hugely popular star of the 1960s, rated by manager Bert Head as his best-ever signing. He is pictured here, in typically assertive action, during a match at Blackpool. John played 229 Palace games, having joined the club from Aberdeen in 1966 for a fee of just £1,500.

Left: Ronnie Allen joined the Palace in 1961, towards the end of a distinguished career both domestically and at international level. He was a supremely talented winger or centre forward and immediately struck up an exciting partnership with Johnny Byrne. However, it was later in his time with Palace that we saw him at his vintage best, as he skippered the club to the 1964 promotion. *Right*: Charlie Catlett was Palace's groundsman at Selhurst Park for thirty-eight years – right from its opening in 1924 – and, as such, remains the longest serving employee of all at Crystal Palace FC.

Crystal Palace directors and management staff, from left to right, front row: Ralph Shrager, Arthur Wait, Victor Ercolani. Back row: Bert Head (Manager), George Petchey (Assistant Manager), Arthur Rowe (Assistant Manager) and Chris Hassell (Secretary). This photograph was taken around the time of Bert Head's appointment in April 1966.

Two more stars of Crystal Palace in the late 1960s – these men both earned a place in any Palace hall of fame. *Left*: Terry Long, the only man to feature in all three promotion seasons of that decade, established a club record 480 League and cup appearances between 1955 and 1968. *Right*: John Sewell, the popular and talented skipper of the Palace team that took the club into the top flight for the first time in 1968/69.

This page shows two of Palace's goals in the 6-0 trouncing of Norwich on Tuesday 16 April 1968 at Selhurst Park. *Above*: The opening strike, netted by Bobby Woodruff (partly hidden behind the near post) after just three minutes. *Below*: Tommy Vansittart, playing in only his fifth game, adds to the lead barely three minutes later, after the Norwich 'keeper had fumbled a Steve Kember drive.

Palace are defending in this action shot from the FA Cup third round tie against Charlton at The Valley on Saturday 4 January 1969. The Palace players (in the dark shirts) are, from left to right: John Loughlan, Roger Hoy and John McCormick; they are repelling the Addicks' raid, led by Ray Treacy, Graham Moore and Paul Went.

Palace's first home game of 1968/69 was against Huddersfield on Wednesday 14 August, a match which they won 2-1. This picture shows (from left to right) John McCormick, Cliff Jackson (behind the goalkeeper) and Steve Kember, watching an early effort sizzle just wide of The Terriers' goal.

MATCH DETAILS

...ult: Palace...... Opponents......
...hins. Palace...... Opponents......
...rers: Palace ....

....

Opponents ....

....

...stitutes: Palace .... minutes

.... for ....

Opponents ...... minutes

.... for ....

...endance: ....

...er Details: ....

Programme No. 11   Saturday, 2nd November, 1968   Kick-off 3.00 p.m.

CRYSTAL PALACE   VERSUS   BOLTON WANDERERS

Shirts: Claret with thin light Blue Stripes
Shorts: White
Stockings: Light Blue with Claret Tops

Football League Div. 2

Today's match ball has been kindly donated by

Mr. P. D. Bosworth
23 Pleasant Grove,
Shirley, Croydon.

Referee:
K. H. BURNS
Stourbridge

Linesmen:
C. I. Boswell
Gillingham
(Cerise Flag)
L. J. Davies
Ammanford, Wales
(Orange Flag)

Shirts: White
Shorts: Blue
Stockings: White

Crystal Palace	Bolton Wanderers
1. John JACKSON	1. Eddie HOPKINSON
2. Roger HOY	2. John RITSON
3. John LOUGHLAN	3. Sid FARRIMOND
4. David PAYNE	4. Gareth WILLIAMS
5. John McCORMICK	5. John HULME
6. Mel BLYTH	6. David HATTON
7. Mark LAZARUS	7. Terry WHARTON
8. Steve KEMBER	8. Fred HILL
9. Cliff JACKSON	9. Roy GREAVES
10. Bobby WOODRUFF	10. Brian BROMLEY
11. Colin TAYLOR	11. Gordon TAYLOR
12. John SEWELL	12. Dave LENNARD

The centre pages of the Palace programme for 1968/69 (shown approximately half the actual size). The Palace line-up shows all the heroes of that terrific season, whilst Bolton's side includes Gordon Taylor, the current secretary of the Professional Footballers Association.

No picture of Bert Head could be too big and no praise too high for the man who led Crystal Palace into Division One for the first time in 1968/69 – and who kept us there for four seasons.

Steve Kember has just netted against Middlesborough on the damp afternoon of Saturday 4 May 1968, but it is evident from his reaction (or lack of it) and that of the Palace men behind him, that the goal has been disallowed because of an infringement.

Left: Whilst the long throw-in is an accepted feature of the modern game, it was a rarely used weapon in the late 1960s and Bobby Woodruff's prodigious efforts were hugely effective. *Right:* The Palace defenders, (from left to right) John McCormick, Mel Blyth and Roger Hoy, put tremendous pressure on the Bristol City rearguard in the match at Selhurst Park on Saturday 19 October 1968, in which Palace came from behind to win 2-1.

John McCormick was dominant in the air and obdurate on the ground. He was at the heart of the Palace defence throughout 1968/69 and is seen here relieving a potentially dangerous situation in the game at Portsmouth on Saturday 28 September 1968, a match which finished 3-3.

This picture became quite famous at the time it was first published – for obvious reasons. The camera has caught the ball directly in front of the Palace player's face during the home game against Bury on Saturday 15 March 1969, a match which finished 1-0. The player is, as contemporary fans may remember, Steve Kember and he is being harried by the Shakers' left-back, Michael Saile.

Mark Lazarus was Palace's powerful, raiding winger in thirty-eight League matches in 1968/69. He hit eleven goals in that promotion campaign and Palace supporters at that time loved his exuberant celebratory tours after he had scored, in which even the policemen were not exempt from his embrace!

Cliff Jackson in action against Middlesborough in the epic Good Friday clash between the promotion contenders on 4 April 1969, a game that finished goal-less. The structure of the Arthur Wait Stand can be seen taking shape in the background.

Catch the mood! Even though it was thirty years ago, it isn't difficult to enter into the jubilation at Selhurst Park as Palace players and fans celebrate our arrival in the top flight, having beaten Fulham 3-2 on Saturday 19 April 1969. John Jackson holds aloft the champagne, flanked by John McCormick and Cliff Jackson.

Six
Palace Gain
Another Title
1969-79

Crystal Palace Football Club, 1979/80. The squad are proudly displaying the old Division Two Championship Cup. From left to right, back row: Dave Horn (Trainer), Gerry Francis, Billy Gilbert, Dave Swindlehurst, Terry Boyle, Ian Walsh, Charlie Simpson (Physiotherapist). Middle row: Alan Harris (Coach), Tony Hazell, Mike Elwiss, Peter Nicholas, Terry Fenwick, Jerry Murphy, Ernie Walley (Reserve Team Coach), Terry Venables (Manager). Front row: Tony Sealy, Steve Kember, John Burridge, Jim Cannon, David Fry, Ken Sansom, Vince Hilaire.

For 1969/70, Palace relied on a blend of the best of the men from the promotion-winning side of the previous season and several new signings. Steve Kember, who represented the former category, is seen here eluding Bobby Moncur of Newcastle in the 0-3 defeat at Selhurst Park on Saturday 4 October.

The best of the new players was Gerry Queen, an ace Scottish striker from Kilmarnock. He topped the Palace scoring chart with eleven League and cup goals.

Alan Birchenall added further zest to Palace's attack in 1970/71 and he is seen here heading their second goal in the 3-2 victory over Stoke City on Saturday 3 April at Selhurst Park.

Left: Skipper John Sewell and Phil Hoadley ensure that Tony Brown of West Bromwich Albion can find no way through during Palace's 3-0 victory on Saturday 17 October 1970. *Right*: Birchenall in action again, this time against Derby County on Saturday 12 December. Although he appears to have beaten the Rams' skipper, Dave Mackay, and goalkeeper, Les Green, the header was off target and the game ended goal-less.

During the seasons in which Crystal Palace have been in the top flight, matches against the football giants of Liverpool have had a special savour for players and fans alike. This page shows scenes from two of the early clashes. *Above left*: Palace's captain for the day, Peter Wall, shakes hands with his former colleague, Tommy Smith, before the contest at Selhurst Park on Saturday 16 January 1971. *Above right*: Alan Birchenall beats the Reds' 'keeper, Ray Clemence, and defender, Chris Lawler, to head down a cross from John Sewell which (below) Gerry Queen slotted into the net, despite a fierce challenge from Larry Lloyd.

The match was tense, tight… and tough. Alan Birchenall receives solace from his team-mates after a bruising challenge, while the Liverpool defenders look on with disdain. However, Palace's 1-0 victory made it all worthwhile!

This picture is from Liverpool's visit to Selhurst Park on the second Saturday of the 1972/73 season (19 August) and shows Peter Wall heading what seemed to be a certain Liverpool goal off the line during the first half – to the evident relief of Mel Blyth. This match ended 1-1.

This picture, from the Rob Marsden collection, is of the Palace match at Wolves on the dismal afternoon of Saturday 30 January 1971. From left to right, Gerry Queen, John Sewell, Kenny Hibbitt, Frank Munroe, Terry Wharton and Alan Birchenall watch Bernard Shaw's header repel a Palace attack in the 1-2 defeat.

Palace's first match of the 1970/71 season was at The Hawthorns, where they held West Bromwich Albion to a 0-0 draw. Here, Palace's Peter Wall admires John McCormick's domination of John Talbut.

Palace defenders Mel Blyth and Bobby Bell watch John Jackson deal capably with this Everton attack, spearheaded by Joe Royle, during the FA Cup third round replay at Goodison Park on the evening of Tuesday 18 January 1972 – a game that Palace lost 2-3.

In October 1971, Palace boss Bert Head took drastic transfer action to remedy a poor start to the season. Favourites Alan Birchenall and Steve Kember left the club for big fees to fund several newcomers, four of whom are seen here, from left to right: striker John Craven (from Blackpool), defenders Bobby Bell (Blackburn) and Sammy Goodwin (Airdrie), and Bobby Kellard, who rejoined the club from Leicester.

The two pictures on this page show just how astute Bert Head's signings had been. *Above*: Bobby Kellard sends Bob Wilson, the Arsenal 'keeper, the wrong way from the penalty spot on Tuesday 11 April 1972. This goal sparked a comeback that saw Palace recover from 0-2 down after four minutes, John Craven heading the equalizer on the hour. *Below*: Willie Wallace (far left), who had joined Palace from Celtic, despatches the goal that earned Palace a point from the visit of Ipswich to Selhurst Park on Saturday 13 November 1971.

This superb photograph of Bobby Tambling depicts one of the game's great craftsmen and strikers of the period. He initially signed for Palace on loan in January 1970, but joined the club permanently six months later. He played eighty League and cup games for Palace, scoring twenty goals: curiously, most of these were scored on opponents' grounds. His best remembered goal is perhaps the successfully converted penalty that ensured Palace's first-ever victory at Highbury in a League Cup replay in November 1970 (picture courtesy of Fotosports).

THE GLAZIERS
CRYSTAL PALACE F.C.

WOLVERHAMPTON WANDERERS

FOOTBALL LEAGUE DIVISION ONE
SATURDAY 10 MARCH 1973
OFFICIAL CLUB PROGRAMME INCLUDING 'LEAGUE FOOTBALL' PRICE 7p

This front cover of a Palace matchday programme from the 1972/73 season reflects the strip favoured by the club at that time and incorporates the club crest. The back was unusual too – pictures of the Palace players surrounded a central block of text listing the opposing line-up.

The last six months of 1972/73 will always be remembered for the explosive arrival of striker Don Rogers and the mayhem he caused amongst top-flight defences. *Above*: Don is starting on one of his runs, attended by Dave Webb, in the match at Chelsea on Saturday 25 November 1972 – a game which finished 0-0. *Below*: Don rounding Alex Stepney of Manchester United, to score Palace's third goal in a 5-0 rout on Saturday 16 December 1972.

Malcolm Allison started as Palace's manager on Saturday 31 March 1973. His arrival inspired the team to their first victory over London opponents in thirty-two top-flight games between 1969 and 1973, but he was unable to prevent Palace being relegated. Unfortunately, worse was to follow.

John Jackson, Palace's outstanding goalkeeper throughout the club's top-flight tenure of 1969-73, left the club in October 1973. Although perhaps equalled by Nigel Martyn twenty years later, he was certainly never bettered by another Palace 'keeper. Jackson's contribution of 393 senior Palace appearances remains unsurpassed by any other goalkeeper at the club.

The high point of Malcolm Allison's career as Palace manager was the FA Cup run of 1975/76, in which The Eagles reached the semi-finals for the first time in their history. Here is some dramatic action from the sixth round victory at Sunderland on 6 March. Peter Wall (far left) and Ian Evans (far right), watch Jim Cannon dive full length to repel an attack by the Wearsiders.

By this time, Palace were in Division Three. They had been relegated for the second year running in 1974, although a great escape had seemed possible after a fine 3-1 victory at Fulham on Good Friday 12 April. However, Palace lost the next three games, including the return against Fulham the following Tuesday evening and it was all to no avail. This picture shows Jeff Johnson (4) crowning the occasion with his second and Palace's third at Craven Cottage.

Terry Venables took over as Palace manager on 15 June 1976. Within three years he had led Palace to two promotions and the Division Two championship.

Peter Taylor had been Malcolm Allison's best signing for Palace, but he moved to Tottenham for £200,000 early in 1976/77, after gaining The Eagles' first full England international cap in over half a century.

Striker Jeff Bourne was the signing who lifted The Eagles from also-rans to successful promotion contenders. He scored nine goals from fifteen games in the spring of 1977, including two in the fabulous 4-2 victory at Wrexham in the last match of the season – a result that ultimately clinched Palace's promotion at the Welshmen's expense.

David Kemp was another Palace striker. He was at his most prolific in the early months of 1975/76, his first full season with the club, when his goals took Palace to the top of the Division Three table.

Two scenes from Palace's 1976/77 promotion season. *Above*: Ian Evans (far right) is about to score Palace's first goal at Brighton in an FA Cup first round tie on Saturday 20 November. Ricky Heppolette (behind the goalkeeper) and Dave Swindlehurst are also in the thick of the action. *Below*: Jim Cannon (left) sets up a Palace attack for Paul Hinshelwood and Nicky Chatterton at Preston on Saturday 16 October – a game that The Eagles lost 1-2.

Palace's unluckiest player in 1978/79 was Mark Elwiss, the record-signing striker, seen here against Sheffield United at Bramall Lane on Saturday 2 September – a game that Palace won 2-0. Mike limped off at Cambridge, just before Christmas, with an injury that spelt the end of his Palace career.

Under the scrutiny of Nick Chatterton and Ian Evans, Rachid Harkouk rounds Nigel Batch, Grimby's goalkeeper, during a 2-1 Palace win on Saturday 15 January 1977. 'Eagle' eyed readers will notice that the Mariners are wearing Palace's second strip of red and blue stripes.

Ian Walsh matured to provide a useful addition to the Palace strike force in the 1978/79 assault on the Division Two title. Among his eight goals was the opener in the titanic climax against Burnley, when a 2-0 Palace win secured the championship.

Vince Hilaire's graceful, mercurial skills were a delight to the football purist and he was seen at his best in Palace's championship season of 1978/79. In total he made 293 appearances for The Eagles between 1977 and 1984.

Goalkeeper John Burridge (right) and left-back Kenny Sansom (below) formed part of the defence that is, statistically speaking, the best in Palace's history, as it conceded only twenty-four goals in the entire 1978/79 promotion campaign. 'Budgie' went on to have a prodigious career which spanned nearly thirty seasons and over a score of clubs. Kenny was, quite simply, the best left-back the club has ever had – as testified by his nine full caps for England gained whilst a Palace player.

Palace opened 1978/79 with a tough away game at Blackburn on Saturday 19 August and gained a creditable 1-1 draw. This picture shows Nick Chatterton taking on three Rovers defenders, with Dave Swindlehurst (far left) and Paul Hinshelwood on hand.

Jerry Murphy is seen here in typical action. His sophisticated left foot is in creative mode; his socks are rolled down and Palace are going forward.

Billy Gilbert partnered Jim Cannon in all but
two of Palace's fixture's in 1978/79 and made
an ideal foil for the experienced captain.

Dave Swindlehurst was Palace's top scorer
in both the 1976/77 and 1978/79
promotion seasons and he netted the first
and last goals in the latter campaign to
help The Eagles secure the championship.

Ian Walsh soars to deliver a flying header in the re-arranged fixture at Newcastle on the evening of Wednesday 7 April 1979, the 0-1 defeat being Palace's only loss in the twenty games after Boxing Day.

Seven
Eagles on the Ebb
1979-84

Crystal Palace Football Club, 1982/83 season. From left to right, back row: Ken Shellito (Assistant Manager), Henry Hughton, Billy Gilbert, Ian Edwards, Paul Barron, David Fry, Gary Williams, Tommy Langley, Steve Lovell, Brian Bason, Alan Mullery (Manager). Front row: Steve Galliers, Shaun Brooks, Kevin Mabbutt, Jim Cannon, Paul Hinshelwood, Jerry Murphy, David Giles.

Palace made a steady, then impressive, entry into the top-flight in 1979, when we were particularly strong at home. *Above*: Terry Fenwick winning a heading duel in the 2-0 victory over Aston Villa on Saturday 15 September. *Below*: New signing Mike Flanagan ran riot and scored twice against Derby County in the 4-0 victory two weeks later.

Clive Allen came to Crystal Palace from Arsenal in August 1980. He began his Palace career in great style, notching the club's first top-flight hat-trick in the 5-2 defeat of Middlesborough on 23 August (the match shown in the picture). However, regrettably, he soon lost his zest for the game whilst at Palace and joined Terry Venables at Queens Park Rangers the following summer.

'Is that clear enough for you ref!' Here is Clive Allen's goal-that-never-was at Coventry on Saturday 6 September 1980, when his crashing, rising drive rebounded so quickly from the stanchion that the officials never saw it and the referee refused to allow it! However, Neil Everitt's superb photograph is conclusive. In one sense this was the defining moment of 1980/81 for Crystal Palace, because nothing went right for The Eagles after it and we were relegated in disarray the following May. Palace fans at the game were astonished at the decision, all the more so since it was evident from the reaction of the Coventry players that they had conceded a goal. We were also irritated (to say the least) by the cavalier attitude of Coventry chairman Jimmy Hill on television later that weekend: 'These things happen in soccer' he said dismissively. Would the pundit have been so offhand if Coventry had suffered in this way?

Ron Noades, former chairman of
Wimbledon, took over Crystal Palace on 26
January 1981 and eventually became
Palace's longest-serving post-war holder of
that office.

Palace were back in Division Two
for the 1981/82 season. This picture
shows Ian Walsh turning Sheffield
Wednesday defender Rav
Blackhall, in Palace's single-goal
defeat at Hillsborough on Saturday
5 September.

Manager Alan Mullery took charge at Crystal Palace in June 1982. His appointment was a controversial one because he had been a fierce opponent of Palace, especially during his time at rivals Brighton. Regrettably, his two years at the Palace helm were bitterly disappointing and ineffectual.

Peter Nicholas, magnificent as a driving, defensive midfield player in Palace's 1978/79 championship-winning side, rejoined the club in October 1983, via a complex loan agreement, from Arsenal. His tenacity and experience were invaluable in The Eagles quest for Division Two survival during that difficult season. Now Palace's youth team manager, Eagles fans have always regarded Peter with affection and respect.

Striker Kevin Mabbutt joined Palace in October 1981, but was one of the most unlucky footballers of his generation. A very gifted player, with a fine future in prospect, he suffered two serious injuries with Palace, the second of which effectively ended his career. Kevin is seen here in action against Blackburn Rovers on Saturday 7 November, a game that Palace lost 1-2.

Goalkeeper George Wood was probably Alan Mullery's best signing for The Eagles. He had a deserved reputation as a top-ranking custodian and demonstrated his class and skill to Palace fans for four and a half years, accumulating 221 senior appearances and seldom missing a match. His 100 consecutive appearances, straight from his debut, were the first at the Palace for over a quarter of a century and have not been equalled since.

Steve Coppell became Palace's manager in June 1984. Formerly a brilliant, penetrative right-winger with Manchester United and England, his playing career was cut short by a crippling knee injury. In two spells at the Palace helm, he became the club's most successful manager of all time and is now The Eagles' respected director of football, based at Strete Court.

Gary Locke was a thoroughly steady and reliable right-back, who made 101 appearances for Palace in the mid-1980s. He also played in the centre of defence as his career drew to a close. Gary is seen here firing home a stunning goal for The Eagles, which enabled them to grab a point from his former club, Chelsea, during a 2-2 draw in November 1982.

Big striker Trevor Aylott was Steve Coppell's first signing for The Eagles. Powerful and whole-hearted, though not a prolific scorer, Trevor topped Palace's scoring chart in his first season with the club with nine goals. He is seen here with Steve Dowman of Charlton Athletic, during a Division Two match at The Valley on Easter Saturday 6 April 1985, a game that finished 1-1.

Phil Barber was originally a striker, but increasingly featured on the left side of midfield. He started every game of Palace's 1988/89 promotion season in that position and only an injury in the first top-flight game the following season prevented him from completing full appearances in that term too. Phil ultimately played 288 matches for the Palace and scored forty-one goals.

Fabulous goal – fabulous picture! In fact, Neil Everitt received an award for this magnificent action shot of the goal scored by Jim Cannon with a flying header. This strike was the only successful one during the game against Middlesborough at Selhurst Park on Saturday 4 May 1985 and the win ensured Palace's Division Two survival.

Eight

The Steve Coppell Years 1984-90

Crystal Palace Football Club, 1988/89. From left to right, back row: Gavin Nebbeling, Phil Barber, Perry Suckling, Brian Parkin, Mark Harris, Neil Redfearn. Middle row: Steve Coppell (Manager), Mark Bright, Jeff Hopkins, Geoff Thomas, Gary O'Reilly, Dave Madden, Dennis Bailey, David Burke, Ian Evans (Assistant Manager). Front row: John Pemberton, Glenn Pannyfather, Alan Pardew, Ian Wright, John Salako.

These two pages depict four Crystal Palace stars of the middle to late 1980s. *Above*: Mighty Micky Droy in acrobatic action at Shrewsbury on Sunday 18 August 1985 – a game Palace won 2-0. Steve Ketteridge is the player watching the action. *Below*: Andy Gray.

Ace winger Alan Irvine, whose game was all about pace, trickery and refinement, is eluding Franz Carr and Johnny Method during one of an extraordinary series of cup ties between Palace and Nottingham Forest, which were a marked feature of the period.

Mark Bright, who developed into a fabulous striker and scored 113 goals for The Eagles.

Two great club servants at Crystal Palace. *Left*: Jim Cannon, player of the year in 1986/87. Jim was the only Palace man ever to win this prestigious award three times and is the leading appearance holder for the club by a long way, with 663 senior games. *Below*: Len Chatterton, who was the groundsman at Selhurst Park from 1966 until 1987 and was the reserve team manager for eight seasons before that. Len had even played on the wing for Palace in the early 1940s and has fronted the Junior Eagles organisation with distinction since his retirement.

The Palace programme in the late 1980s featured occasional cartoons by local graphic designer Phil Dunster, himself an ardent Palace fan for many years. This one was Phil's response to The Eagles 5-1 demolition of hapless Plymouth on Saturday 3 November 1987.

Here's the other half of Palace's lethal scoring duo of the late 1980s – Ian Wright. *Above*: Ian is netting the only goal of a 1-0 victory over West Bromwich Albion on Saturday 29 April 1989, during the run-in to the promotion season. *Below*: Ian causing further consternation to the Blackburn defence in the second leg of the play-off final at Selhurst Park on Saturday 3 June 1989 – which Palace ultimately won 3-0 to claim promotion with a 4-3 aggregate score.

Jeff Hopkins was Steve Coppell's most expensive signing outside the top-flight, but the tribunal-fixed fee of £240,000 was an investment, as Jeff was the captain of the 1988/89 promotion-winning team as well as a creditable performer in Division One the following season.

Ian Wright again, this time stabbing the ball past Terry Gennoe for Palace's first goal in the play-off final second leg at Selhurst Park against Blackburn.

Steve Coppell receives the acclaim of Palace fans after The Eagles' victory over Blackburn had assured a return to Division One.

David Madden's contribution to Palace's 1989 promotion was considerably greater than the statistics indicate. He played in less than half the matches and scored just six goals but, just at the crucial time, Dave assumed responsibility from the penalty spot and converted the five spot-kicks Palace were awarded during the run-in at the end of the season. This photograph was taken after the one he successfully converted early in the second half of the play-off final to level the aggregate score.

Nigel Martyn became the nation's first £1 million goalkeeper when he joined Palace in November 1989 from Bristol Rovers. He made an immediate impact, starring in the side which earned the club its first appearance in an FA Cup final, then became part of the best-ever top-flight defence the Palace have boasted, in 1990/91. In 1992, Nigel gained full international recognition and, ultimately, made 349 senior appearances for The Eagles, where he is rated as the greatest goalkeeper, alongside John Jackson.

Alan Pardew joined the Palace from Yeovil Town in March 1987 and was another brilliant signing by Steve Coppell. He missed only one match in The Eagles' (extended) 1988/89 promotion-winning season, but it was 1989/90 that Palace fans will remember him for – turn the page to see 'Super-Al' in historic action and find out the reason why!

Alan Pardew heads Palace's fourth goal, during extra-time, to defeat Liverpool in the FA Cup semi-final at Villa Park on Sunday 8 April 1990.

Mark Bright watches Palace's opening goal in the epic 1990 FA Cup Final against Manchester United at Wembley on Saturday 12 May. The dramatic encounter finished with honours even at 3-3.

'Brighty' turns away, his delight shared by the Palace fans behind the goal.

Another angle on the goal, scored with a looping header from Gary O'Reilly (out of picture) after a quarter of an hour, following a Phil Barber free-kick on the right flank.

The 1990 FA Cup Final against Manchester United went to a replay, which sadly ended in a 0-1 defeat, the following Thursday evening. Palace fans were at Wembley in full strength and provided wonderful visual and vocal support, in spite of the fact that the game was dour and uncompromising. Palace wore a yellow and black strip for this match and the picture shows skipper Geoff Thomas in a midfield tussle with United's Paul Ince, under the gaze of Richard Shaw.

Nine
Wembley Regulars
1990-98

Crystal Palace Football Club, 1994/95. From left to right, back row: Spike Hill (Kit Manager), Paul Sparrow, Glen Little, Eric Smith, Peter McLean (Physiotherapist). Third row: Kevin Hall, Brian Launders, George Ndah, Eddie Dixon, Andy Preece, Ian Cox, Andy Thorn, Bobby Bowry, Ricky Newman, Jamie Vincent, Tony Scully. Second row: David Kemp (Assistant Manager), Bruce Dyer, Darren Patterson, Damian Matthew, Dean Gordon, Jimmy Glass, Nigel Martyn, Richard Shaw, Darren Pitcher, Paul Williams, Ray Lewington (Coach). Front row: John Salako, John Humphrey, Chris Armstrong, Ray Wilkins, Alan Smith (Manager), Gareth Southgate, Chris Coleman, Simon Rodger, Eric Young.

Palace returned to Wembley on Sunday 7 April 1991 to win the Full Members Cup, beating Everton 4-1 after extra-time. The photograph shows John Salako scoring Palace's third goal.

During the early 1990s, the rivalry with Liverpool swung decisively in Palace's favour. This photograph and those on the opposite page are from three fabulous victories over the Merseyside giants. The above picture shows Mark Bright's goal, which assured victory at Selhurst Park, on Sunday 30 December 1990.

Geoff Thomas' downward header provides the Palace winner at Anfield on Saturday 2 November 1991. Marco Gabbiadini (10), who had scored the equalizer, looks on.

Andy Thorn is delighted after his extra-time winner at Selhurst Park in a League Cup fourth round replay on Wednesday 16 December 1992.

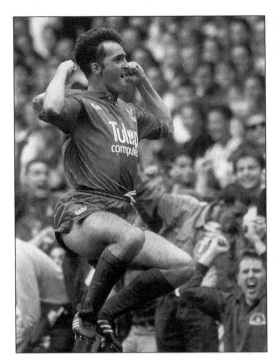

Winger (or sweeper) Eddie McGolderick (above left) and right-back John Humphrey (above right) were regular members of Palace teams and firm favourites with fans in the early 1990s.

The tension of the occasion of the meeting between relegation-threatened sides, in this case Palace and Middlesborough, at Selhurst Park on Saturday 11 April 1993, shows in the faces of Chris Coleman (left) and Curtis Fleming. Palace's 4-1 victory consigned 'Boro to the drop, but ultimately both clubs lost their Premiership status.

Giant central defender Eric Young created a club record of full international caps gained whilst on Palace's books, with nineteen appearances for Wales. Eric played 204 times for The Eagles, including full appearances in the 1993/94 Division One championship season.

Left: Tall, stylish Alan Smith took over as Palace manager in June 1993, after nearly ten years previous service to the club. He immediately led The Eagles back into the Premier League. *Right:* Paul Stewart spent three highly productive months with Palace in early 1994, whilst on loan from Liverpool. It was a brilliant ploy, as he proved to be the catalyst that turned Palace into the best side in Division One and ensured not just promotion, but the championship as well.

Chris Armstrong was Palace's top scorer in the 1993/94 championship side and is shown here completing his hat-trick on Saturday 28 August 1993, when Palace defeated Portsmouth 5-1.

The packed Holmesdale Road terracing, when the final match of the season – a 0-2 defeat by Watford on Sunday 8 May 1994 – provided 'The Last Stand' at Selhurst Park.

Chris Armstrong again, with another headed goal, this time against Liverpool in a 1-6 defeat on Saturday 20 August 1994.

The 1994/95 season contained little for Palace fans to savour, but its highlight was unquestionably the 2-1 victory over Arsenal at Highbury on Saturday 1 October. The picture shows Palace's superb skipper, Gareth Southgate, in contention with Arsenal's Stefan Schwarz.

The Holmesdale Road stand was erected between May 1994 and August 1995 at a cost of some £6 million.

Left: Palace chairman Ron Noades is joined by Steve Coppell to perform the opening ceremony for the new stand, prior to Palace's game against Charlton – which finished as a 1-1 draw – on Saturday 26 August 1995. *Right:* Dave Bassett was installed as Palace's manager on 8 February 1996.

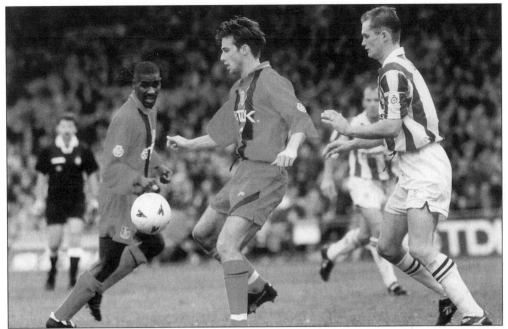

Palace's Dougie Freedman shields the ball from Huddersfield captain Lee Sinnott in the goal-less draw at Selhurst Park on Saturday 16 September 1995.

Left: Bruce Dyer, who moved to Barnsley for £750,000 in October 1998, possessed pace, strength and exuberance during his time at Selhurst. He was the club's top scorer in 1996/97, with seventeen Division One goals. *Right*: Local boy Dean Gordon matured through the Palace youth scheme to become The Eagles' most-capped player for England at under-21 level, with thirteen international appearances.

Two of the stars of Palace's 1996/97 season. *Left*: David Hopkin was the skipper of the side and scored the vital Wembley winner that secured promotion. *Right*: Neil Shipperley, who made his debut against Grimsby on Saturday 26 October 1996, scored thirteen goals from thirty-five appearances in Division One that season.

Jubilation knew no bounds after the Wembley play-off final victory!

Foreign players became a major feature at the Palace during the troubled 1997/98 season. Attilio Lombardo (top left), Sasa Curcic (top right) and Herman Hreidarsson (below left) all performed creditably for the club, but the player of the year was Marc Edworthy (bottom right).

Incredibly, Palace went through to mid-April before winning a home game in the 1997/98 Premiership. Perversely, they had won the 'away' game against Wimbledon at Selhurst Park on 20 September. Attilio Lombardo is pictured here, striking the only goal of the game.

Left: Paul Warhurst has just scored against Bolton in the 2-2 draw on 27 September. *Right:* Italian international striker Michele Padavano.

Ten

Back to the Future
1998

Crystal Palace Football Club 1998/99. From left to right, back row: Neil Shipperley, David Tuttle, Valerian Ismael, Clinton Morrison, Bruce Dyer, Andy Linighan, Herman Hreidarsson, David Woozley, Richard Harris, Andrew Frampton. Third row: Gary Sadler, Bobby Armit (Physiotherapists), James Hibbert, Sasa Curcic, Nicky Rizzo, Pablo Rodgrigues, Tony Folan, Hayden Mullins, Andrew Martin, Gareth Graham, Wayne Carlisle, Murray Jones (Youth Team Coach), Stuart Scott (Youth Team Coach). Second row: Dr Bill Jasper, John Cartwright (CPFC Academy Director), Steve Kember (Reserve Team Coach), Terry Fenwick (First Team Coach), David Amsalem, Jamie Fullarton, Gareth Ormshaw, Lee Kendall, Kevin Miller, Fraser Digby, Steve Thomson, Kieron Loughran, David Butler (Coach), Simon Little (Masseur), Vic Bettinelli (Kit Manager). Front row: Ted Buxton (Personal Assistant), Paul Warhurst, Attilio Lombardo, Matthew Jansen, Marcus Bent, Terry Venables (Manager), Marc Edworthy, Dean Austin, Jamie Smith, Simon Rodger, Peter Nicholas (Youth Team Manager).

Left: The Eagles' new manager for 1998/99 was the highly successful former Palace and England boss, Terry Venables. *Right:* Skilful Yugoslavian international midfielder Sasa Curcic was a huge favourite among Palace fans and frequently deployed as a highly effective sustitute.

Striker Bruce Dyer in League Cup action against Torquay in one of his last games for Palace before his move to Barnsley. Brucie netted forty-four goals during his 164 appearances for Palace.

Matt Jansen was one of Palace's brightest stars in the first half of 1998/99, during which he attracted the interested of many Premiership sides. Blackburn Rovers finally secured his services in January for £4.1 million. He is pictured here eluding a challenge from a Norwich City opponent during Palace's terrific 5-1 victory over The Canaries on 17 October – a match in which he scored two goals.

Left: Among Palace's multi-national team of 1998/99 were two players from China, the first men from that country to play senior football in Britain. Palace fans quickly took Fan Zhiyi and Sun Jihai (pictured here) to their hearts. *Right:* Attilio Lombardo in action at West Bromwich Albion, a 2-3 defeat for Palace, on 3 November 1998.

There was intense media coverage of the arrival of Palace's Chinese players in August 1998. Here, Fan (right) and Sun pose patiently for the cameras.

Powerful Australian international Craig Foster made his debut against Ipswich on 30 September 1998. He captained the team before Christmas.

Midfielder Hayden Mullins proved to be the discovery of 1998/99. A product of the Palace youth scheme, he made his debut in the opening game of the season and regularly demonstrated neat passing ability, creativity and a high work rate.

Left: Clinton Morrison became Palace's first teenage striker to net on his Premiership debut, when he scored with his first touch in the last game of 1997/98. He confirmed his progress as a useful member of the Palace squad in 1998/99 with an important goal in the 4-2 defeat of Bury on 30 September. He is pictured here in action against Watford on 28 November. *Right:* Matt Jansen ponders The Eagles' prospects as the season advances.

Acknowledgements

Every modern day Crystal Palace follower knows the extent of the club's debt to ace photographer Neil Everitt for his stunning – and sometimes award-winning – pictures, that so greatly enhance every Palace publication. This book is no exception, and I should like to place on record my own gratitude to Neil for those which are used in this book to such positive effect.

In addition, I greatly appreciate the help of another of my long-standing Palace friends, Ian King, who supplied several pictures of our former ally and Eagles enthusiast, Rob Marsden: every reader will enjoy the quality of these pictures and a complimentary copy of the book has been sent to Rob's widow to mark my appreciation.

Thank you too, to all those Palace supporters who, upon hearing of the forthcoming production of this book, encouraged me in writing it with their enthusiasm for the project.

Finally, all who care for the image and reputation of Crystal Palace Football Club will join me in thanking Tempus Publishing, and their sports editor James Howarth in particular, for including this book in their *Archive Photographs* series and making such an attractive product out of it. The Eagles may not have won as many honours as some other outfits but, when it comes to the quality of our publications, no-one betters us!

Nigel Sands
January 1999